Guided Reading Notes

Dark Blue Band
Oxford Level 15

Endangered

Contents

Introduction	2
The Swarm (Fiction)	6
Piranha! (Fiction)	13
Big Game Adventure (Fiction)	20
The Amazon (Non-fiction)	27
Facing Danger (Non-fiction)	34

Introduction

Why is guided reading important?

Guided reading plays an important role in your whole-school provision for reading, providing opportunities for children to progress and develop the key competencies they need to become confident and skilled independent readers. Working with small groups of children, with texts closely matched to the readers' needs, guided reading is the perfect vehicle for delivering focused teaching from Reception/PI right through to Year 6/P7. The teacher-pupil interaction also provides a valuable assessment opportunity, helping you identify exactly what each child can and can't do. Through guided reading children also encounter a world of exciting, whole books – building a community of readers who read for pleasure.

About *Project X Origins*

Project X Origins is a comprehensive, whole-school guided reading programme designed to help you teach the wide range of skills essential to ensure children progress as readers and to help nurture a love of reading.

Ensuring the key skills are covered

Project X Origins incorporates all of the key skills children need to develop to become successful and enthusiastic readers:

> **Word reading:** phonically regular and common exception words are introduced systematically in the early levels with phonic opportunities provided throughout the notes. As children progress, they are encouraged to use their decoding skills whenever they encounter new or unfamiliar words, and also to recognize how this impacts on different spelling rules.

- **Comprehension:** understanding what has been read is central to being an effective and engaged reader but comprehension is not something that comes automatically so specific strategies have been built into the notes to ensure children develop comprehension skills they can use over a range of texts:

  - Previewing
  - Predicting
  - Activating and building prior knowledge
  - Questioning
  - Recalling
  - Visualizing and other sensory responses
  - Deducing, inferring and drawing conclusions
  - Determining importance
  - Synthesizing
  - Empathizing
  - Summarizing
  - Personal response, including adopting a critical response

- **Reading fluency:** fluency occurs as children develop automatic word recognition, reading with pace and expression. Strategies to help achieve this, including meaningful opportunities for oral reading, re-reading and re-listening are provided throughout.

- **Vocabulary:** introducing new vocabulary within a meaningful context is an important element in extending children's vocabulary range, developing their reading fluency and comprehension. Each thematic cluster provides opportunities for revisiting and reinforcing vocabulary over a range of books and contexts.

- **Grammar, punctuation and spelling:** learning about language in the context of a text, rather than through a series of discrete exercises, can help make grammar, punctuation and spelling relevant and helps children make the link between grammar, punctuation and clarity of meaning, thus supporting their development as writers. Opportunities to support an in-depth look at language are provided for every book from Year 1/P2 to Year 6/P7.

- **Spoken language:** talk is crucial to learning and developing their comprehension so children are given plenty of opportunities to: discuss and debate their ideas with others; justify their opinions; ask and answer questions; explore and hypothesise; summarise, describe and explain; and listen and respond to the ideas of others.

Assessment and progression in reading

Project X Origins includes a rigorous assessment spine drawn from the *Oxford Reading Criterion Scale* to ensure that you know exactly what each child can do and what they need to focus on next in order to make progress. This assessment framework, combined with the careful levelling of the Oxford Levels, will help you select the right book with the right level of challenge for each of your guided reading groups and to assess, track and monitor each child's progress.

Step 1

On a termly basis, use the *Oxford Reading Criterion Scale* (which can be found in the relevant *Project X Origins Teaching Handbook*) to assess each child's reading. The scale will tell you the Oxford Level a child is comfortable reading at, and the areas a child needs to develop. You can also use this assessment to form your guided reading groups.

Step 2

Plan your guided reading sessions by selecting books at the appropriate Oxford Level that focus on the relevant learning needs of the group. You will find charts showing the learning objectives and assessment points for every *Project X Origins* book in the relevant *Project X Origins Teaching Handbook*. Depending on your assessment, you might choose a book at the level the children are comfortable at or one from the next level up, to offer some stretch.

Step 3

Use the assessment points within the Guided Reading Notes to support on-going assessment of children's reading progress. The Progress Tracking Charts in the relevant *Project X Origins Teaching Handbook* can be used to record this if you wish. Regularly re-assess each child's progress combining your on-going informal assessments and the termly assessment using the *Oxford Reading Criterion Scale*. Use this information to re-organize guided reading groups and teaching plans in response to children's varying degrees of progress.

Getting started: using the Guided Reading Notes

At a glance
Project X Origins Guided Reading Notes offer detailed guidance to help deliver effective and engaging guided reading sessions, and are designed to be used flexibly to ensure you get the most out of each book. For notes containing multiple sessions, you may choose to focus on each of these sessions or focus on one session and have the children read the rest of the book independently.

Curricular correlation and assessment
At the beginning of every set of notes there are correlation charts for all UK curricula, ensuring that across the clusters the main curricular objectives are covered. In addition, an overview of assessment points for each book is provided – these points are also signposted throughout the notes.

Key information
Before the first session, an overview of the book and the resources you will need (such as additional photocopy masters) is provided.

Teaching sequence
Each guided reading session follows the same teaching sequence:
- **Before reading**: children explore the context of each book to support their understanding and help them engage with the text. They are encouraged to discuss, recall, respond, predict and speculate about the book. Opportunities to focus on word reading and/or vocabulary are also introduced at this point.
- **During reading**: children are given a section of the book to read with specific questions in mind.
- **After reading**: children reflect on and discuss what they have read. They are encouraged to delve deeper, exploring their understanding of the text, developing their vocabulary, grammar, punctuation, spelling and fluency where appropriate.
- **Follow-up**: opportunities for children to extend their learning outside the session are provided, including writing and cross-curricular activities.

Throughout the sessions, the key strategies that children are developing are clearly identified.

The Swarm
BY MARTYN BEARDSLEY

Curricular correlation

English National Curriculum

Spoken language	Ask relevant questions to extend their understanding and knowledge
Word reading	Apply their growing knowledge of root words, prefixes and suffixes (morphology and etymology), both to read aloud and to understand the meaning of new words that they meet
	Read further exception words, noting the unusual correspondences between spelling and sound, and where these occur in the word
Comprehension	Discuss words and phrases that capture the reader's interest and imagination
	Draw inferences such as inferring characters' feelings, thoughts and motives from their actions, and justifying inferences with evidence
	Participate in discussion about both books that are read to them and those they can read for themselves, taking turns and listening to what others say

Developing grammar, punctuation, vocabulary and spelling

Grammar and Punctuation	Fronted adverbials	At that moment, the intercom buzzed.
Vocabulary and Spelling	Endings which sound like /shun/, spelt *-tion, -sion, -ssion*	collision, directions, instructions, mentioned, confusion, explanation
	Challenge and context words	hypnotized, mayhem, rhythmical, coordinates, shimmered

Reading assessment points (Oxford Reading Criterion Scale: Assessment Standard 5)

2. Can the children read confidently and independently using a range of strategies appropriately to establish meaning? (READ)
3. Can the children skim read texts to gather the general impression of what has been written? (R)
4. Can the children scan texts to locate specific information? (R)
9. Can the children read some Y4/5 high frequency words? (READ)
12. Are the children able to quote directly from the text to support thoughts and discussions? (R)
13. Can the children work out the meanings of ambitious words and/or phrases in context? (D)
17. Can the children identify the effects of different words and phrases to create different images and atmosphere? (E)
23. Can the children sometimes explain different characters' points of view?(D)

Scottish Curriculum for Excellence

Listening and talking	I can select ideas and relevant information, organise these in an appropriate way for my purpose and use suitable vocabulary for my audience LIT 2-06a
Reading	I can select and use a range of strategies and resources before I read, and as I read, to make meaning clear and give reasons for my selection LIT 2-13a
	To show my understanding, I can respond to literal, inferential and evaluative questions and other close reading tasks and can create different kinds of questions of my own ENG 2-17a
	I can discuss the writer's style and other features appropriate to genre ENG 2-19a
	I can make notes, organise them under suitable headings and use them to understand information, develop my thinking, explore problems and create new texts, using my own words as appropriate LIT 2-15a

Programme of Study for English in Wales

Oracy	Organise talk so that different audiences can follow what is being said (Speaking)
Reading	Contribute to group discussion and help everyone take part (Collaboration)
	Identify how texts differ in purpose, structure, layout (Reading strategies)
	Skim to gain the gist of a text or the main idea in a chapter (Reading strategies)
	Use a range of strategies to make meaning from words and sentences, including knowledge of phonics, word roots, word families, syntax, text organisation and prior knowledge of context (Reading strategies)
	Accurately identify the main points and supporting information in texts (Comprehension)
	Deduce connections between information, e.g. sequence, importance (Comprehension)

Northern Ireland Curriculum

Talking and Listening	Share, respond to and evaluate ideas, arguments and points of view and use evidence or reason to justify opinions, actions or proposals
Reading	Use a range of cross-checking strategies to read unfamiliar words in texts
	Consider, interpret and discuss texts, exploring the ways in which language can be manipulated in order to affect the reader or engage attention
	Begin to be aware of how different media present information, ideas and events in different ways, for example, compare and contrast two characters in a story or history text

Session 1 (Chapter 1)

About this book
Team X travel to the Western Sahara Desert where the Collector is taking bees from all across the world in order to shrink them for his collection. Team X use their bee-machines to get closer to the bees and save the day!

You will need
- *Vocabulary bookmark* Photocopy Master, *Teaching Handbook* for Year 5/P6
- *What are they thinking, feeling, saying?* Photocopy Master, *Teaching Handbook* for Year 5/P6
- *NICE 'Mission Accomplished' report* Photocopy Master, *Teaching Handbook* for Year 5/P6

▸ Before reading

- Discuss the title of the story. What is a swarm? Read the blurb on the back cover. If the children have already met one of the snow globe stories in Project X, remind them of what the Collector was trying to achieve. If not, talk about what a snow globe is. **(activating prior knowledge)**
- Read page 3. Ask the children how they think the Collector might be involved with this story. **(predicting)**
- Remind the children what to do if they encounter a difficult word, or if they struggle to understand the meaning of a word or a sentence.

▸ During reading

- Ask the children to read to the end of Chapter 1.
- As they read, ask them to notice how the author emphasizes words and ideas through the use of repetition and italics.
- Ask the children to note any new or unusual words and record these on their *Vocabulary bookmark* Photocopy Master. Ask them to write down their own definitions of these words.

Assessment point
Can the children read confidently and independently using a range of strategies appropriately to establish meaning?
(ORCS Standard 5, 2)

▸ After reading

Returning to the text
Ask the children:
- What have the characters found out in this chapter? Encourage the children to summarize the main points. **(recall, summarizing)**

- What ideas do you think the characters might have about why the bees are vanishing? **(inferring)**
- What impact could the loss of bees have on the environment? **(inferring, activating prior knowledge)**

The author's craft

- What authorial technique does the author use in the first paragraph to help the reader realize that Rita Motherwell is an expert on bees? (repetition of the words *she knew*)

> **Assessment point**
> Can the children identify the effects of different words and phrases to create different images and atmosphere?
> (ORCS Standard 5, 17)

Developing comprehension

- Ask the children to suggest how Rita Motherwell might have felt at the point where she lifted her veil. **(deducing, inferring, drawing conclusions)**
- Ask them to complete the *What are they thinking, feeling, saying?* Photocopy Master for Rita at this point in the story. **(empathizing)**

> **Assessment point**
> Can the children sometimes explain different characters' points of view?
> (ORCS Standard 5, 23)

Developing vocabulary

- Share the words the children have recorded on their bookmarks. Look at them in context and check that the children understand their meaning.
- Ask them to compare their own definitions with a dictionary.

> **Assessment point**
> Can the children work out the meanings of ambitious words and/or phrases in context?
> (ORCS Standard 5, 13)

Session 2 (Chapters 2 and 3)

Before reading

- Ask the children to recap briefly the story to date. **(recall)**
- Look at the title of Chapter 2. What do the children think the 'breakthrough' might be? **(predicting)**

- Before children read independently, ask them to rehearse what to do if they become stuck on a word or sentence.

During reading

- Ask the children to read Chapters 2 and 3.
- As they read, ask them to notice the different ways the author has chosen to present information in these chapters, e.g. a map, a newspaper article and a note.
- Ask the children to find words and phrases the author uses to convey uncertainty and possibility, e.g. *might*, and note them down as they read.

After reading

Returning to the text

Ask the children:

- What was inside the parcel? **(recall)**
- How did the snow globe give a clue to the whereabouts of the bees? **(recall)**
- What do you think the bee-machines look like? **(visualizing)**
- How has the author used Tiger's dialogue on page 15 to show his character? **(inferring)**

Assessment point

Are the children able to quote directly from the text to support thoughts and discussions? (ORCS Standard 5, 12)

The author's craft

- Ask the children to look at the length of the sentences in Chapter 3. What do they notice?
- How has the author built up suspense and pace?

Assessment point

Can the children identify the effects of different words and phrases to create different images and atmosphere? (ORCS Standard 5, 17)

Developing comprehension

- Ask the children to quickly sketch a possible design for a bee-machine. What features is it likely to need? **(visualizing)**

> ### Developing grammar, punctuation and spelling
>
> - Ask the children to share the words and phrases they have found that convey uncertainty and possibility. Explain that these are modal verbs (auxiliary verbs), like *might* or *will*, or adverbs, like *possibly*.
> - Where modal verbs are used, remind children that these will be followed by a main verb.
> - Ask children to choose a sentence containing one of their example words or phrases and to change the modal verb/adverb. How does this affect the meaning?

- Prior to Session 3, ensure the children have read Chapters 4 and 5 independently.

Session 3 (Chapters 6)

Before reading

- Ask the children to tell you what has happened so far. **(recall)**
- Ask them to describe the waggle dance (some children may like to act it out). **(recall)**
- Before children read independently, ask them to rehearse what to do if they become stuck on a word or sentence.

During reading

- Ask the children to read Chapter 6 and to the end of the story.
- Point out the word *collision* on page 32. Ask the children to note other words that end with the /shun/ sound as they read.
- As they read, ask them to reflect on their feelings about the story. **(personal response)**

> **Assessment point**
> Can the children read some Y4/5 high frequency words?
> (ORCS Standard 5, 9)

After reading

Returning to the text

- Ask the children what they think of the story. What parts did they particularly like/dislike? **(personal response, adopting a critical stance)**
- Extend this activity by asking the children to write a review of the book. **(personal response)**

The Swarm

Developing comprehension

- Ask the children to note down the main points of the story. Ask them to use these to retell orally the story as if they were a newsreader reporting the events. **(visualizing, determining importance, summarizing)**

Assessment point

Can the children skim read texts to gather the general impression of what has been written? (ORCS Standard 5, 3)

Can the children scan texts to locate specific information? (ORCS Standard 5, 4)

Developing grammar, punctuation and spelling

- Look at the words *direction* and *confusion*. Explain that it can be difficult to know which spelling to use for the /shun/ sound. If the root word ends *-t* or *-te* they should use *-tion*, if it ends *-d*, *-de* or *-se*, they should use *-sion*.

Writing opportunities

- Look at the picture and the heading 'Meanwhile in the Collector's hideout…' on page 46. Ask the children to write this chapter from the Collector's point of view.

Follow-up

Writing activities

- Write a full news report of the events in the story. **(longer writing task)**
- Write an email to Charles Sting about the adventure. **(short writing task)**
- Write the end of mission report on the *NICE 'Mission Accomplished' report* Photocopy Master. **(longer writing task)**

Further literacy activities

- Record the children's news reports. **(spoken language)**

Cross-curricular activities

- Research the life cycle of bees. **(Science)**
- Design and perform a waggle dance. **(PE)**
- Design and make a bee-machine. **(DT)**

Piranha!
BY JAN BURCHETT AND SARA VOGLER

Curricular correlation

English National Curriculum

Spoken language	Participate in discussions, presentations, performances, role play/improvisations and debates
Word reading	Apply their growing knowledge of root words, prefixes and suffixes (morphology and etymology), both to read aloud and to understand the meaning of new words that they meet
	Read further exception words, noting the unusual correspondences between spelling and sound, and where these occur in the word
Comprehension	Participate in discussions about both books that are read to them and those they can read for themselves, taking turns and listening to what others say

Developing grammar, punctuation, vocabulary and spelling

Grammar and Punctuation	Use of paragraphs to organise ideas around a theme	
Vocabulary and Spelling	Words with 'silent' letters	designed, climbed, doubts, guests
	Challenge and context words	tambaqui, piranha, deforestation, destruction, foliage

Reading assessment points (Oxford Reading Criterion Scale: Assessment Standard 5)

2. Can the children read confidently and independently using a range of strategies appropriately to establish meaning? (READ)
5. Can the children use text marking to support retrieval of information or ideas from texts, e.g. highlighting, notes in the margin? (R)
8. Can the children use clues from action, description and dialogue to help establish meaning? (D)
12. Are the children able to quote directly from the text to support thoughts and discussions? (R)
14. Can the children read between the lines, using clues from action, dialogue and description to interpret meaning and/or explain what characters are thinking/feeling and the way they act? (D)

Scottish Curriculum for Excellence

Listening and talking	When I engage with others, I can respond in ways appropriate to my role, show that I value others' contributions and use these to build on thinking LIT 2-02a
Reading	I can select and use a range of strategies and resources before I read, and as I read, to make meaning clear and give reasons for my selection LIT 2-13a
	To help me develop an informed view, I can identify and explain the difference between fact and opinion, recognise when I am being influenced, and have assessed how useful and believable my sources are LIT 2-18a
	I can discuss the writer's style and other features appropriate to genre ENG 2-19a
	I regularly select and read, listen to or watch texts which I enjoy and find interesting, and I can explain why I prefer certain texts and authors LIT 2-11a

Programme of Study for English in Wales

Oracy	Explain information and ideas using supportive resources (Speaking)
Reading	Contribute to group discussion and help everyone take part (Collaboration)
	Use a range of strategies to make meaning from words and sentences, including knowledge of phonics, word roots, word families, syntax, text organisation and prior knowledge of context (Reading strategies)
	Explore information and ideas beyond their personal experience (Comprehension)
	Identify how texts differ in purpose, structure and layout (Reading strategies)

Northern Ireland Curriculum

Talking and Listening	Identify and ask appropriate questions to seek information, views and feelings
Reading	Use a range of cross-checking strategies to read unfamiliar words in texts
	Justify their responses logically, by inference, deduction and/or reference to evidence within the text, for example, compare and contrast two characters in a story or history text

Session 1 (Chapters 1–2)

About this book

Dani discovers a worrying drop in Tambaqui fish in a lake in the Amazon rainforest. Team X set off to investigate. They find the cause of the problem – piranha fish invading the water. Soon they discover that the famous celebrity chef, Mortimer Scoffer, has cooked up an interesting recipe for his new Sushi restaurant.

You will need

- *Vocabulary bookmark* Photocopy Master, *Teaching Handbook* for Year 5/P6
- *Five senses* Photocopy Master, *Teaching Handbook* for Year 5/P6
- *Compare and contrast* Photocopy Master, *Teaching Handbook* for Year 5/P6
- *Delectable Dining Den recipe* Photocopy Master, *Teaching Handbook* for Year 5/P6

Before reading

- Look at the front cover. What do the children know about piranha fish? Where do they come from? What is special about them? **(activating prior knowledge, encouraging reflection)**
- Look at page 4. What do they know about the Amazon Rainforest? What 'human activity' is threatening the area? **(activating prior knowledge, previewing)**
- Ask the children how they think the chef mentioned on page 3 might be linked to the Amazon. **(predicting)**
- Remind the children what to do if they encounter a difficult word, or if they struggle to understand the meaning of a word or a sentence.

During reading

- Ask the children to read Chapters 1 and 2.
- As they read, ask them to note any new or unusual words. They could record these on the *Vocabulary bookmark* Photocopy Master.

Assessment point

Can the children read confidently and independently using a range of strategies appropriately to establish meaning?
(ORCS Standard 5, 2)

After reading

Returning to the text

Ask the children:

- What strategies did you use to read the word *tambaqui*? Look at page 8. What do the authors do to help the reader to pronounce the word accurately?

- Using the information on page 8 and the knowledge that you have about piranha fish, what conclusions can you draw about what could be the possible problem with the tambaqui fish in this story? **(deducing, inferring and drawing conclusions)**
- What type of vehicle is the Green Dart? **(recall)**
- What does amphibious mean and what other words have a similar derivation? **(deducing)**
- Ask the children to take up freeze-frame positions of the characters in the scene when the goliath bird-eating spider confronts their Green Dart on page 14. Tap each child on the shoulder and ask them what they are thinking. **(empathizing, inferring)**

The author's craft

- What do the children notice about Cat and Tiger's response to Max on page 6 when he asks if the chef is the one who uses all the weird ingredients? Why have the authors given the two characters the same response? Ask the children to read this section using the appropriate expression that shows how one word (*Exactly*) can have different meanings. **(deducing, inferring and drawing conclusions)**
- Discuss how the authors use the characters' dialogue to develop characterisation and build drama.

Assessment point

Can the children read between the lines, using clues from action, dialogue and description to interpret meaning and/or explain what characters are thinking/feeling and the way they act? (ORCS Standard 5, 14)

Developing comprehension

- Read the non-chronological reports on the tambaqui (p.8) and the goliath bird-eating spider (p.16). How might they be linked within the story? **(predicting, deducing, inferring and drawing conclusions)**
- Ask the children to imagine what it was like for the characters when they landed in the jungle. They could use the *Five senses* Photocopy Master to help them.

- Prior to Session 2, ensure the children have read Chapters 3–4 independently.

Session 2 (Chapter 5)

▶ Before reading

- Ask the children to recap briefly the story to date. **(recall)**
- Look at the title of Chapter 5. Who do the children think Harriet Spatula might be? **(predicting)**
- Before the children read independently, ask them to rehearse what to do if they become stuck on a word or sentence.

▶ During reading

- Ask the children to read Chapter 5.
- On page 34, point out *doubts* and ask the children to pronounce the word. Ask the children to note any other words with silent letters as they read.
- As they read, ask them to notice how Tiger's perceptions of the chef change.

> **Assessment point**
> Can the children use text marking to support retrieval of information or ideas from texts?
> (ORCS Standard 5, 5)

▶ After reading

Returning to the text

Ask all the children:

- What does Harriet Spatula hate and how might this have an impact on the story? **(recall, inferring)**
- Why is it Mortimer Scoffer's most important night? Why is he concerned about Harriet Spatula? **(recall, inferring)**
- Why are all the piranha in the lake? **(recall)**

> **Assessment point**
> Can the children quote directly from the text to support thoughts and discussion?
> (ORCS Standard 5, 12)

Developing comprehension

- Use the pictures of the restaurant on pages 25, 26–27 and 38 and the descriptions in the text to draw conclusions about the type of restaurant this is. What might it be like to eat here? **(deducing, inferring)**
- Using the *Compare and contrast* Photocopy Master, ask the children to compare this restaurant with one that they are familiar with.

Assessment point
Can the children use clues from action, description and dialogue to help establish meaning?
(ORCS Standard 5, 8)

Developing grammar, punctuation and spelling

- Ask the children to share the words with silent letters they have found.

Session 3 (Chapter 6)

Before reading

- Ask the children to talk about what has happened in the story. **(recall)**
- Reread page 36 from *He's such a creep!* Allow the children time to think of a plan that Max might have in mind for thwarting Scoffer's chances of receiving a good restaurant review by Harriet Spatula. The children then take it in turns to be Max to be interviewed by the other children in the group. **(questioning, deducing, predicting)**
- Before the children read independently, ask them to rehearse what to do if they become stuck on a word or sentence.

During reading

- Ask the children to read to the end of Chapter 6.
- As they read, ask them to look out for commands or instructions, e.g. "*Jump!*" (p.37).
- As they read, ask them to reflect on their own feelings about the story and their overall response to it.

Assessment point
Can the children read confidently and independently using a range of strategies appropriately to establish meaning?
(ORCS Standard 5, 2)

After reading

Returning to the text

- What do the children think of the story? **(personal response)**
- Do they feel that Mortimer had his 'just rewards'?
- Can they identify any underlying moral to the story?

Developing comprehension

- Ask the children why the authors have written *No piranha were hurt during the making of this book*. Why is this funny? **(inferring)**
- What impact will Harriet Spatula's review have on the chef? **(deducing, inferring and drawing conclusions)**

Assessment point
Can the children use clues from action, description and dialogue to help establish meaning?
(ORCS Standard 5, 8)

Developing grammar, punctuation and spelling

- Look at the commands or instructions the children have found.
- Discuss how the verbs take the imperative form in these sentences and always come at the start of the sentence, e.g. *"Leave it to me,"* (p.40).

Follow-up

Writing activities

- Write a non-chronological report on piranha fish based on the model for tambaqui fish (p.8). **(short writing task)**
- Write a food-critic review of the recipe created in the DT cross-curricular activity using the example on page 46 of the story as a model. **(longer writing task)**

Cross-curricular activities

- Create a picture of the rainforest using Henri Rousseau as a focused artist study. **(Art and Design)**
- Design a recipe using unusual ingredients using the *Delectable Dining Den recipe* Photocopy Master. **(DT)**
- Research the Amazon and the impact of deforestation on the population. **(Geography)**

Big Game Adventure

BY ALISON HAWES

Curricular correlation

English National Curriculum

Spoken language	Articulate and justify answers, arguments and opinions
Word reading	Apply their growing knowledge of root words, prefixes and suffixes (morphology and etymology), both to read aloud and to understand the meaning of new words that they meet
	Read further exception words, noting the unusual correspondences between spelling and sound, and where these occur in the word
Comprehension	Read books that are structured in different ways and read for a range of purposes
	Identify themes and connections in a wide range of books

Developing grammar, punctuation, vocabulary and spelling

Grammar and Punctuation	Use of commas after fronted adverbials	Once they have recovered, After a while, Suddenly, Later
	Appropriate choice of pronoun or noun within and across sentences to aid cohesion and avoid repetition	Mark is pleased he has done something right at last.
Vocabulary and Spelling	The suffix -ous	enormous, tremendous

Reading assessment points (Oxford Reading Criterion Scale: Assessment Standard 5)

2. Can the children read confidently and independently using a range of strategies appropriately to establish meaning? (READ)
7. Can the children refer to the text to support opinions and predictions? (R/D)
12. Are the children able to quote directly from the text to support thoughts and discussions? (R)
15. Are the children beginning to explore potential alternatives that could have occurred in texts (e.g. a different ending), referring to text to justify their ideas? (D)
21. Are the children beginning to identify differences between some different fiction genres? (A)

Scottish Curriculum for Excellence

Listening and talking	When listening and talking with others for different purposes, I can share information, experiences and opinions LIT 2-09a
Reading	I can select and use a range of strategies and resources before I read, and as I read, to make meaning clear and give reasons for my selection LIT 2-13a
	Using what I know about the features of different types of texts, I can find, select and sort information from a variety of sources and use this for different purposes LIT 2-14a
	I can discuss the writer's style and other features appropriate to genre ENG 2-19a
	I regularly select and read, listen to or watch texts which I enjoy and find interesting, and I can explain why I prefer certain texts and authors LIT 2-11a

Programme of Study for English in Wales

Oracy	Explain information and ideas using supportive resources (Speaking)
	After listening, respond, giving views on what the speaker has said (Listening)
Reading	Use a range of strategies to make meaning from words and sentences, including knowledge of phonics, word roots, word families, syntax, text organisation and prior knowledge of context (Reading strategies)
	Identify how texts differ in purpose, structure, layout (Reading strategies)
	Read texts, including those with few visual clues, independently with concentration (Reading strategies)

Northern Ireland Curriculum

Reading	Use a range of cross-checking strategies to read unfamiliar words in texts
	Begin to be aware of how different media present information, ideas and events in different ways, for example, compare accounts in different newspapers
	Consider, interpret and discuss texts, exploring the ways in which language can be manipulated in order to affect the reader or engage attention
	Reconsider their initial response to texts in the light of insight and information which emerge subsequently from their reading

Big Game Adventure

Session 1 (pages 2–9)

About this book

This book is an action-packed story that allows children to select their own mission to save endangered animals and then make decisions about how to help them. An email arrives on Dr Richard Jones' desk asking for help with animals in danger. Unfortunately he has a broken leg and is unable to go, but his sons step in to save the day.

You will need

- *What are they thinking, feeling, saying?* Photocopy Master, *Teaching Handbook* for Year 5/P6
- *Story planning frame* Photocopy Master, *Teaching Handbook* for Year 5/P6

▶ Before reading

- Have the children ever read books or used computer programs which involved making choices? If they haven't, explain how this book works. **(activating prior knowledge)**
- Read the opening pages to the group. Who are the main characters? Look at the map on pages 4 and 5. Ask the children to read about each mission. Which one interests them most? Why? **(previewing)**
- Remind the children what to do if they encounter a difficult word, or if they struggle to understand the meaning of a word or a sentence.

▶ During reading

- Ask the children to read up to page 9.
- As they read, explain to them that they will need to decide which mission they want to go on.

Assessment point

Can the children read confidently and independently using a range of strategies appropriately to establish meaning? (ORCS Standard 5, 2)

▶ After reading

Returning to the text

Ask the children:

- Why couldn't Dr Jones take on the mission to rescue the animals in danger? **(recall)**
- How do you think Dr Jones might have broken his leg? **(deducing, inferring and drawing conclusions)**
- Do you think Mark will read the handbook? Why or why not? **(deducing, inferring and drawing conclusions)**

Assessment point

Are the children able to quote directly from the text to support thoughts and discussions? (ORCS Standard 5, 12)

The author's craft

- Ask the children what is unusual about the tense in which the author has chosen to write pages 2 and 3. Why do they think she has done this?

Developing comprehension

- Role play the scene in which Liam and Mark try to persuade their Dad to let them go on the missions. Encourage the child who is playing Dr Jones to not give in so easily so the rest of the group have to work hard at persuading him. At various points during the role play tap the children on the shoulder and ask them to tell the rest of the group how they are feeling. **(adopting a critical response, empathizing)**
- Ask the children to complete a *What are they thinking, feeling, saying?* Photocopy Master for one of the characters at the same point in the story. **(empathizing)**

- Prior to Session 2, ensure the children have read the pages which relate to the mission they have chosen to follow.

Session 2 (pages 10–50)

Before reading

- Ask the children to describe which mission they chose and why. What was the main decision they had to take? What were the main problems they faced? Were they successful in saving the endangered animal? **(recall, summarizing)**
- If they could have done something differently, what would they have done? **(personal response, including adopting a critical stance)**
- Ask children to read and follow another mission.

During reading

- As they read, ask them to notice how the author conveys the passage of time, e.g. *After a while ...*
- As they read, ask them to look out for the key points in the story when it is important to make decisions.

After reading

Returning to the text

Ask the children:

- What were the key decisions you had to take in this adventure? **(recall)**
- Do you think the outcomes would have been different if Mark had read the handbook? **(deducing, drawing conclusions)**
- How well do Mark and Liam work together? What evidence supports your opinion? **(empathizing, deducing, inferring)**

> **Assessment point**
> Are the children beginning to explore potential alternatives that could have occurred in texts (e.g. a different ending), referring to text to justify their ideas? (ORCS Standard 5, 15)

Developing comprehension

- Looking back over what they have read, what information can the children predict might be in the handbook? **(synthesizing, inferring, predicting)**

Developing grammar, punctuation and spelling

- Discuss how the author conveys the passage of time across paragraphs.
- Ask the children to identify any adverbials of time, e.g. *late in the evening*. Explain that many of these are fronted adverbials (they appear at the start of the sentence).
- Discuss how fronted adverbials are always followed by a comma.

- Prior to Session 3, ensure the children have read the third mission independently.

Session 3 (pages 51–56)

> Before reading

- Ask the children to tell you what happened in the third mission. Were they successful in the adventure? Had they learnt from previous missions? **(recall)**
- Before the children read independently, ask them to rehearse what to do if they become stuck on a word or sentence.

Assessment point

Can the children refer to the text to support opinions and predictions? (ORCS Standard 5, 7)

> During reading

- Ask the children to read to the end of the book.
- As they read, ask them to think about whether reading the handbook beforehand would have helped Mark during his missions.

> After reading

Returning to the text

Ask the children:

- Do you think Mark should have read the handbook before undertaking the adventures? Why didn't he? What does this suggest about his character? **(synthesizing, deducing, inferring and drawing conclusions)**
- Did you enjoy choosing how to follow the story? Would you like to read other books like this? **(personal response)**

> *The author's craft*

- Ask the children to find dramatic phrases in the story, e.g. *Dark clouds are gathering across the sun* (p.12), *A nearby crocodile opens its jaws and shuffles forward* (p.41). Can they identify how the author has built up the tension?

Developing comprehension

- Discuss the features of adventure stories: usually a series of exciting events leads to a high impact resolution; tension is built up in stages with the climax near the end; can take place in any setting where danger is high.

Assessment point
Are the children beginning to identify differences between some different fiction genres? (ORCS Standard 5, 21)

Developing grammar, punctuation and spelling

- Look at the 'Animals in Danger Safety Handbook' on the last few pages of the book. Draw the children's attention to the 'If' statements on pages 54 and 56. Discuss how the comma divides two separate clauses, e.g. *If a baboon bites you, get medical treatment as soon as you can.*
- Show the children how the clauses could be swapped around and the comma removed to read: *Get medical treatment as soon as you can if a baboon bites you.*

Writing opportunity

- Ask the children, in pairs, to plan an adventure story in which opportunities are given for the reader to make decisions about the outcome.

Follow-up

Writing activities

- Ask the children to write the adventure story they planned in Session 3. **(longer writing task)**
- Write a new page on a different animal for the *Animals in Danger Safety Handbook*. **(short writing task)**

Cross-curricular activities

- Design and create a cover for an *Animals in Danger Safety Handbook*. **(Art and Design)**
- Work out the cost of going on a real-life adventure to one of the chosen destinations from the story, using travel brochures with flight and hotel costs. **(Maths)**

The Amazon
BY DEBORAH CHANCELLOR

Curricular correlation

English National Curriculum

Spoken language	Use relevant strategies to build their vocabulary
Word reading	Apply their growing knowledge of root words, prefixes and suffixes (morphology and etymology), both to read both aloud and to understand the meaning of new words that they meet
Comprehension	Distinguish between statements of fact and opinion
	Read books that are structured in different ways and for a range of purposes
	Identify how language, structure and presentation contribute to meaning

Developing grammar, punctuation, vocabulary and spelling

Grammar and Punctuation	Use of paragraphs to organise ideas around a theme	
Vocabulary and Spelling	Prefix *eco-*	ecosystem, ecological, ecotourism
	Challenge and context words	preying, unhinges, reserves, vulnerable

Reading assessment points (Oxford Reading Criterion Scale: Assessment Standard 5)

2. Can the children read confidently and independently using a range of strategies appropriately to establish meaning? (READ)
7. Can the children refer to the text to support opinions and predictions? (R/D)
11. Can the children identify the ways in which paragraphs are linked? (A)
12. Are the children able to quote directly from the text to support thoughts and discussions? (R)
20. Can the children discuss the work of some established authors and know what is special about their work? (E)
24. Can the children compare the structure of different stories to discover how they differ in pace, build up, sequence, complication and resolution? (A)

Scottish Curriculum for Excellence

Listening and talking	To help me develop an informed view, I can distinguish fact from opinion, and I am learning to recognize when my sources try to influence me and how useful these are LIT 2-08a
Reading	I can select and use a range of strategies and resources before I read, and as I read, to make meaning clear and give reasons for my selection LIT 2-13a
	To show my understanding across different areas of learning, I can identify and consider the purpose and main ideas of a text and use supporting detail LIT 2-16a
	Using what I know about the features of different types of texts, I can find, select and sort information from a variety of sources and use this for different purposes LIT 2-14a
	I can make notes, organise them under suitable headings and use them to understand information, develop my thinking, explore problems and create new texts, using my own words as appropriate LIT 2-15a

Programme of Study for English in Wales

Oracy	Explain information and ideas using supportive resourcess (Speaking)
	After listening, respond, giving views on what the speaker has said (Listening)
Reading	Use a range of strategies to make meaning from words and sentences, including knowledge of phonics, word roots, word families, syntax, text organisation and prior knowledge of context (Reading strategies)
	Identify how texts differ in purpose, structure, layout (Reading strategies)
	Scan for specific information using a variety of features in texts (Reading strategies)
	Select and use information and ideas from texts (Response and analysis)

Northern Ireland Curriculum

Talking and Listening	Describe and talk about real experiences and imaginary situations and about people, places, events and artefacts
Reading	Use a range of cross-checking strategies to read unfamiliar words in texts
	Justify their responses logically, by inference, deduction and/or reference to evidence within the text, for example, compare and contrast two characters in a story or history text

Session 1 (pages 2–7)

About this book
This book explores man's impact on the Amazon rainforest. It provides information about the variety of life that exists in the rainforest and how it is affected.

You will need
- *KWL* Photocopy Master, *Teaching Handbook* for Year 5/P6
- *Summarizing* Photocopy Master, *Teaching Handbook* for Year 5/P6
- *Discussion prompt bookmark* Photocopy Master, *Teaching Handbook* for Year 5/P6
- *Non-fiction planning frame* Photocopy Master, *Teaching Handbook* for Year 5/P6
- Individual leaf shapes for children to write vocabulary on

Before reading

- Look at the front cover and discuss the title. Talk about what the children already know about the Amazon. Ask them, in pairs, to start filling in the *KWL* Photocopy Master. Encourage them to create questions they would like to explore. **(activating prior knowledge)**
- Read pages 2 and 3 together and ensure the children understand what the Amazon is, where it is and what makes it special. **(previewing)**
- Remind the children what to do if they encounter a difficult word, or if they struggle to understand the meaning of a word or a sentence.

During reading

- Ask the children to reread pages 2–3 and to the end of page 7.
- Give children leaf shapes, and as they read, ask them to note words that are new, interesting or puzzling. You might like to display these. **(developing vocabulary)**

Assessment point
Can the children read confidently and independently using a range of strategies appropriately to establish meaning?
(ORCS Standard 5, 2)

After reading

Returning to the text

- Ask the children to revisit the questions they created before reading the book. Have they found any answers? Have they generated new questions? Ask them to update their *KWL* grid. **(questioning, recall, synthesizing)**

The Amazon

The author's craft

- Look at pages 2–3 and point out the features of a non-chronological text: has an opening, often general, statement, e.g. *The Amazon rainforest is one of the great wonders of the natural world*; sometimes followed by more a specific classification, e.g. *The Amazon rainforest and river is sometimes called Amazonia*; information about the subject is grouped together logically in paragraphs to make sense and often provides examples.
- Turn to page 26. Discuss the authors choice of language, especially in the opening statement. Discuss how much author's opinion and/or fact. How does this make you feel? Why?

Assessment point

Can the children identify the ways in which paragraphs are linked? (ORCS Standard 5, II)

Developing comprehension

- Ask the children to summarize the information they have read on pages 2–7, using the *Summarizing* Photocopy Master to help them structure their ideas. **(summarizing)**

Developing grammar, punctuation and spelling

- Focus on the word *ecosystem* on page 6, and ask the children to suggest what the prefix *eco-* means (environmentally friendly). Ask the children to make lists of words that use the prefix *eco-* with a partner.
- Ask them to share their lists and provide them with dictionaries to check their meanings.

Writing opportunity

- Ask the children to work with a partner to create a writing frame for writing a non-chronological report, based on the features identified in the text.

Session 2 (pages 8–15)

❯ Before reading

- Briefly discuss the information the children have already read about on the Amazon. **(recall)**
- As they read, ask them to look out for homophones.

❯ During reading

- Ask the children to choose different sections from pages 8–15 to read.
- As they read, explain that they will each tell the group two or three facts they found most interesting in their sections and why.

> **Assessment point**
> Can the children read confidently and independently using a range of strategies appropriately to establish meaning?
> (ORCS Standard 5, 2)

❯ After reading

Returning to the text

- Ask the children to share some of the facts that interested them, saying why. **(recall)**
- Are they able to answer any further questions from their *KWL* grid?
- How do the children feel about the issues surrounding the Amazon rainforest? **(personal response, adopting a critical stance)**

> **Assessment point**
> Can the children refer to the text to support opinions and predictions?
> (ORCS Standard 5, 7)

❯ *The author's craft*

- Look briefly at the balanced argument on page 14. Discuss the features of a balanced discussion: a statement of the issue, e.g. *It has taken only fifty years to destroy over half of the world's rainforests*; statement sometimes includes supporting evidence, e.g. graph; arguments for and against with examples to support them, e.g. quotes.

The Amazon

> **Developing comprehension**
>
> - Ask the children to discuss the viewpoints of Fergus Walker and Paulo Prates. Which person do they have most sympathy for? **(empathizing)**
> - Hand out the *Discussion prompt bookmark* Photocopy Master, and encourage the children to use the prompts in a debate.

- Prior to Session 3, ensure the children have read pages 16–21 independently.

Session 3 (pages 22–29)

Before reading

- Ask the children to share any further information about the Amazon they have read about. What impact is the destruction of the rainforest having on the animals? **(recall)**

> **Assessment point**
> Can the children quote directly from the text to support thoughts and discussions?
> (ORCS Standard 5, 12)

During reading

- Ask the children to read pages 22–29. Explain that these chapters focus on the impact of the destruction of the rainforest on the people of the Amazon.
- As they read, ask the children to look for examples of *which*, *where* and *that*.
- Ask the them to write notes to give an oral summary and to identify the author's point of view. Is she for ecotourism or against it? What information supports this?

> **Assessment point**
> Can the children read confidently and independently using a range of strategies appropriately to establish meaning?
> (ORCS Standard 5, 2)

After reading

Returning to the text

- Ask each child to give a brief summary of what they have read. **(summarizing, determining importance)**
- Ask them to share their thoughts about the author's point of view. **(personal response)**

Developing comprehension

- Ask the children to debate the subject, choosing one side of the argument and referencing the book to back up their argument. (**summarizing, adopting a critical stance**)

Assessment point
Can the children refer to the text to support opinions and predictions? (ORCS Standard 5, 7)

 Developing grammar, punctuation and spelling

- Look at the examples the children have found of *which*, *where* and *that*. Discuss that these words are used to link a relative clause (a type of subordinate clause) to the main clause, e.g. *The reserve will cover 150,000 square kilometres, which is an area larger than England* (p.27).
- Explore rules for when each of these words should be used, e.g. *where* when describing a place.

 Writing opportunity

- Ask them to use their summary notes to write a brief computer-based report on the Amazon. Encourage them to add visual information and combine pages to form a hyperlinked PowerPoint presentation. They can then use this for an oral presentation persuading people to help protect the rainforest. (**synthesizing, determining importance**)

Follow-up

Writing activities

- Research and use the *Non-fiction planning frame* to create a report on one of the endangered animals on pages 18–21. **(short writing task)**
- Make up a story about someone having an adventure in the Amazon. **(longer writing task)**

Other literacy activities

- Continue adding words to leaf shapes to expand on the theme of environmental protection. **(developing vocabulary)**

Cross-curricular activities

- Use the True or False questions on page 30 to design an Amazon-themed board game. **(Maths, DT)**

Facing Danger
BY CHLOE RHODES

Curricular correlation

English National Curriculum

Spoken language	Maintain attention and participate actively in collaborative conversations, staying on topic and initiating and responding to comments
Word reading	Apply their growing knowledge of root words, prefixes and suffixes (morphology and etymology), both to read aloud and to understand the meaning of new words that they meet
	Read further exception words, noting the unusual correspondences between spelling and sound, and where these occur in the word
Comprehension	Read books that are structured in different ways and for a range of purposes
	Retrieve and record information from non-fiction
	Participate in discussion about both books that are read to them and those they can read for themselves, taking turns and listening to what others say

Developing grammar, punctuation, vocabulary and spelling

Grammar and Punctuation	Use of paragraphs to organise ideas around a theme	
Vocabulary and Spelling	The /y/ sound elsewhere than at the end of a word	yachtsman
	Challenge and context words	hypothermia, malaria, amputated, environments

Reading assessment points (Oxford Reading Criterion Scale: Assessment Standard 5)

2. Can the children read confidently and independently using a range of strategies appropriately to establish meaning? (READ)
3. Can the children skim read texts to gather the general impression of what has been written? (R)
4. Can the children scan texts to locate specific information? (R)
8. Can the children use clues from action, description and dialogue to help establish meaning? (D)
10. Can the children use knowledge of text structure to locate information? (A)
11. Can the children identify the ways in which paragraphs are linked? (A)
12. Are the children able to quote directly from the text to support thoughts and discussions? (R)
13. Can the children work out the meanings of ambitious words and/or phrases in context? (D)
14. Can the children read between the lines, using clues from action, dialogue and description to interpret meaning and/or explain what characters are thinking/feeling and the way they act? (D)

Scottish Curriculum for Excellence

Listening and talking	I can select ideas and relevant information, organise these in an appropriate way for my purpose and use suitable vocabulary for my audience LIT 2-06a
Reading	I can select and use a range of strategies and resources before I read, and as I read, to make meaning clear and give reasons for my selection LIT 2-13a
	Using what I know about the features of different types of texts, I can find, select and sort information from a variety of sources and use this for different purposes LIT 2-14a
	To show my understanding across different areas of learning, I can identify and consider the purpose and main ideas of a text and use supporting detail LIT 2-16a
	I can make notes, organise them under suitable headings and use them to understand information, develop my thinking, explore problems and create new texts, using my own words as appropriate LIT 2-15a

Programme of Study for English in Wales

Oracy	Explain information and ideas using supportive resources (Speaking)
	Contribute to group discussion and help everyone take part (Collaboration)
Reading	Use a range of strategies to make meaning from words and sentences, including knowledge of phonics, word roots, word families, syntax, text organisation and prior knowledge of context (Reading strategies)
	Identify how texts differ in purpose, structure, layout (Reading strategies)
	Scan for specific information using a variety of features in texts (Reading strategies)
	Show understanding of main ideas and significant details in texts, e.g. mindmapping showing hierarchy of ideas, flowchart identifying a process (Comprehension)

Northern Ireland Curriculum

Talking and Listening	Tell, retell and interpret stories based on memories, personal experiences, literature, imagination and the content of the curriculum
Reading	Use a range of cross-checking strategies to read unfamiliar words in texts
	Use traditional and digital sources to locate, select, evaluate and communicate information relevant for a particular task

Facing Danger

Session 1 (pages 2–9)

> **About this book**
> Our world is full of dangers. This book explores the extremes in Earth's nature – hot deserts and jungles, freezing environments, treacherous storms and weather – and follows the exploits of six adventurers who have encountered these dangers and survived.
>
> **You will need**
> - *Vocabulary word map* Photocopy Master, *Teaching Handbook* for Year 5/P6
> - *Newspaper report frame* Photocopy Master, *Teaching Handbook* for Year 5/P6
> - Atlases

▸ Before reading

- Look at the front cover and discuss the title. Talk about why some people have the compulsion to 'face danger'. **(activating prior knowledge)**
- Read pages 2 and 3 together and ensure the children understand that these people have chosen to face these extreme environments and have spent many months or even years preparing themselves. Discuss any stories they may already know from books or films related to facing anger. **(activating prior knowledge)**
- Remind the children what to do if they encounter a difficult word, or if they struggle to understand the meaning of a word or a sentence.

> **Assessment point**
> Can the children read confidently and independently using a range of strategies appropriately to establish meaning?
> (ORCS Standard 5, 2)

▸ During reading

- Ask the children to reread pages 2–3 and then to the end of page 7.
- As they read page 5, ask them to look out for devices that make the paragraph more cohesive, e.g. *so*.
- As they read, ask them to note the key points of Tony Bullimore's recount.

> **Assessment point**
> Can the children identify the ways in which paragraphs are linked?
> (ORCS Standard 5, 11)

▸ After reading

Returning to the text

- Ask the children to summarize Tony Bullimore's recount. **(summarizing)**

The author's craft

- Look at page 5 and point out the features of this explanation: *why* =in the title indicates that the text will explain why something happens; series of logical steps explaining why being cold can be dangerous; uses present tense; includes causal connectives to explain cause and effect.
- Highlight the causal language in the text, e.g. *As your muscles get cold ... move more slowly*; *When the body starts to lose heat ... nose and cheeks get cooler*, etc.

 ### Developing comprehension

- Check the children's understanding of the explanation by asking them to explain orally how frostbite occurs. Allow the children time to do this in pairs, before presenting their explanations to the group. **(recall, visualizing and other sensory responses)**

 ### Developing grammar, punctuation and spelling

- Ask the children to share the words and phrases they noted to link information within paragraphs. What were the words they found? How do they help the reader? Are there similarities between them in terms of where they come within a sentence and what punctuation marks surround them?

- Prior to Session 2, ensure the children have read pages 8–11 independently.

Session 2 (pages 12–15)

Before reading

- Ask the children to recap briefly on any information read so far. **(recall)**
- Before the children read independently, ask them to rehearse what to do if they become stuck on a word or sentence.

During reading

- Ask the children to read pages 12–15. Explain that they will give a summary to the group of what they have read.
- On page 12, point out *tsunami* and ask the children to pronounce the word.
- Ask the children to note any other words with silent letters as they read.

> **Assessment point**
> Can the children clarify the meanings of ambitious words and/or phrases in context? (ORCS Standard 5, 13)

After reading

Returning to the text

- Go round the group asking each child to give a brief oral summary of what they have read in the section about the Asian tsunami. **(recall, summarizing, determining importance)**
- Model making brief summary notes as they talk, listing the page number and the key points.
- Ask them to use an atlas to track the course of the tsunami, locating places referred to in the text.

> **Assessment point**
> Can the children use knowledge of text structure to locate information? (ORCS Standard 5, 10)

Developing grammar, punctuation and spelling

- Ask the children to share the words with silent letters they have found.

- Prior to Session 3, you may wish the children to read pages 16–25.

Session 3 (pages 26–29)

▶ Before reading

- Discuss dilemmas. Have the children ever faced a dilemma? What did they do? Did anyone help them to decide what to do? Was it a difficult decision they had to make? Why? **(activating prior knowledge)**
- Before the children read independently, ask them to rehearse what to do if they become stuck on a word or sentence.

▶ During reading

- Ask the children to read pages 26–27 only.
- As they read, ask them to consider the range of emotions going through the two men's minds.

Assessment point

Can the children read between the lines, using clues from action, dialogue and description to interpret meaning and/or explain what characters are thinking/feeling and the way they act? (ORCS Standard 5, 14)

Can children use clues from action, description and dialogue to help establish meaning? (ORCS Standard 5, 8)

▶ After reading

Returning to the text

- Ask the children to describe the features of the Rescue reports on pages 7 and 15: key facts have been extracted using skimming and scanning to enable the reader to get a quick summary of the text.

Assessment point

Can the children skim read texts to gather the general impression of what has been written? (ORCS Standard 5, 3)

Can the children scan texts to locate specific information? (ORCS Standard 5, 4)

▶ *Developing comprehension*

- Discuss Simon's decision. What would the children have done? Was he right or wrong? **(empathizing, personal response, including adopting a critical stance)**
- Now ask the children to read Joe's story on page 28. Does Joe's view of the situation make a difference to how the children feel about Simon? If so, what has changed their minds? **(adopting a critical stance)**

Assessment point

Are the children able to quote directly from the text to support thoughts and discussions? (ORCS Standard 5, 12)

Writing opportunity

- Without looking at the one on page 29, ask the children to write a Rescue report for Joe and Simon's account in the style of the others, then compare the reports. **(summarizing)**

Follow-up

Writing activities

- Complete the *Vocabulary word map* Photocopy Master for some of the new vocabulary encountered in this book. **(short writing task)**
- Use the *Newspaper report frame* Photocopy Master to create a news item about one of the accounts in the book. **(short writing task)**
- Make up a survival story about one of the explorers on pages 16–17, editing it to include the facts. **(longer writing task)**

Cross-curricular activities

- Locate the countries that contain deserts, mountains or rainforests. **(Geography)**
- Compare styles of different landscape artists, such as Turner, Utagawa Hiroshige and modern artists like Kyffin Williams. **(Art and Design)**
- Use the skills listed in the third column of the Survival Skills table on page 30 to discuss the attributes which help people to survive in dangerous situations. **(PSHE)**